THE VIOLENT EARTH
EARTHQUAKE

JOHN DUDMAN

Wayland

Titles in this series

Earthquake
Flood
Storm
Volcano

Editor: Sarah Doughty
Designer: Tony Truscott
Artist: Nick Hawken
Consultant: Sandy Lawson,
engineering seismologist

First published in 1992 by
Wayland (Publishers) Ltd
61 Western Road, Hove
East Sussex, BN3 1JD, England

**British Library Cataloguing in
Publication Data**
Dudman, John
  Earthquake.—(The violent earth)
  I. Title II. Series
  551.22

HARDBACK ISBN 0-7502-0364-1

PAPERBACK ISBN 0-7502-1319-1

Typeset by Tony Truscott Designs
Printed in Italy by Rotolito Lombarda S.p.A.

Picture: Relief workers survey the wreckage
of old wooden houses in San Francisco after
the earthquake struck in 1989.

CONTENTS

A survivor remembers

Marcela Gomez, aged ten, was at Sunday school with her five year old brother in Chimbote, a port in Peru, when the ground started to tremble violently. Later she remembered, 'I grabbed his hand and we ran out into the street. All of a sudden, he left me and ran back inside. He yelled that he had forgotten his bag of sweets in the broken building. The noise was terrible. There was a lot of dust, clouds of it everywhere. The dust wrapped around my little brother... I don't remember anything else.'

What happened in Peru

Marcela was among the few people who escaped injury in Chimbote on 31 May 1970 when the earthquake struck the Andean mountains overlooking the coast of Peru. More than 300 people died in Chimbote and thousands were hurt. Buildings collapsed as a sudden release of energy underground made the earth roll like ocean

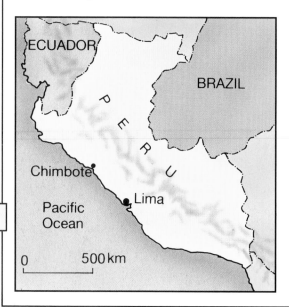

waves. But although the port was shattered it was only a tiny part of the disaster.

The earthquake's violence
The earthquake was so violent that it measured almost 8 on the Richter scale (the scale used to measure earthquakes). Rocks and mudslides fell on to towns and villages as the earthquake tore away a mountainside. A lake spilled over its bank and turned into a waterfall of death.

About 50,000 people were killed and thousands more were injured. More than 800,000 people were made homeless. Big earthquakes like this one are not unusual in some parts of the world. So what is it that causes the earth to shake so violently?

A deserted village in Peru after the 1970 earthquake. (Inset) Earthquake survivors receiving aid.

5

WHY EARTHQUAKES HAPPEN

Inside the earth

The centre of the earth is an inferno, which is so hot the surrounding rocks melt. These rocks are part of the enormous plates which lie beneath the outer crust of our planet.

The plates are always moving. Landmasses are made of light material and rest on the moving plates.

For hundreds of millions of years, big areas of land and ocean have been slowly changing shape as the underground plates slide, grind and scrape against each other. Today, this activity still goes on. Where the earth's crust is thin, weak, or cracked such as on some mountain ranges, the heat from inside the earth sometimes comes out in volcanic explosions.

Below: Earthquakes occur mostly at the plate edges where pressure builds up. One plate may be forced to move below the edge of another causing an earthquake shock.

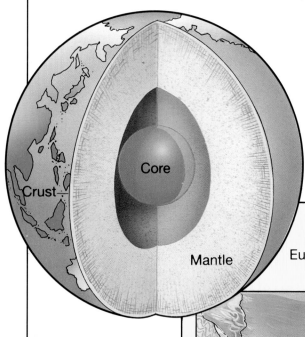

Above: A section through the earth showing the crust, the mantle, and the fiery core.

Core

Crust

Mantle

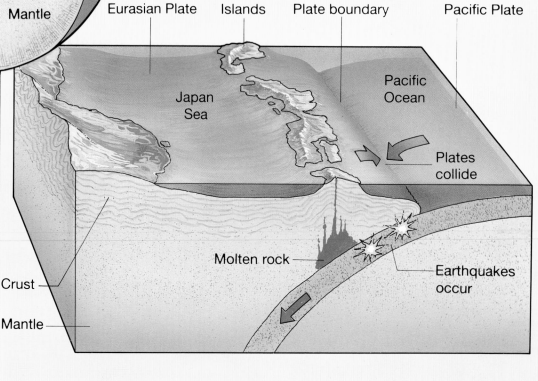

Eurasian Plate   Islands   Plate boundary   Pacific Plate

Japan Sea

Pacific Ocean

Plates collide

Molten rock

Earthquakes occur

Crust

Mantle

Faulting

Earthquakes are also caused by the movement of the plates. The plates scrape against each other at the plate boundaries. This builds up pressure which becomes so strong that it makes the rocks break along a fracture, or fault. This causes a powerful jolt or earthquake shock. The shock waves travel outwards from the focus, which is where most of the movement takes place. The point on the earth's surface above where the earthquake occurs is called the epicentre. This is where most of the damage caused by the earthquake takes place.

Mechanism of earthquakes

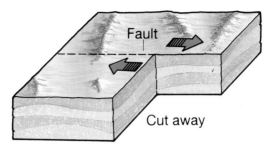

1. Rock is pushed and pulled along fault line.

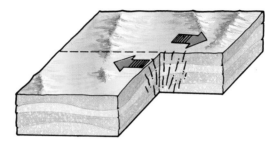

2. Cracks develop in rock.

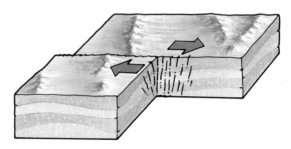

3. Rocks break along fault line.

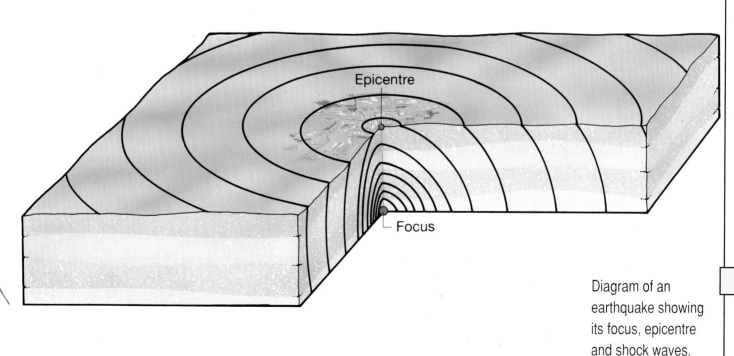

Diagram of an earthquake showing its focus, epicentre and shock waves.

The dangerous boundaries

More than 300,000 earthquakes whose tremors can be felt occur every year. Others are only slight tremors which are too light to be noticed. Only a few earthquakes cause major disasters.

In some parts of the world, earthquakes are more likely to happen than in others. The dangerous places for people to live are the areas that lie along the boundaries, or edges of the earth's plates. These areas have very active faults. There is a pattern of more than twenty plate edges which are known to be earthquake zones. Some of these edges follow the coastlines of continents. Others meet beneath oceans and mountain ranges.

Below: The 'Ring of Fire' circles the Pacific Ocean from New Zealand up to Japan, crosses eastwards and passes down the coasts of North and South America.

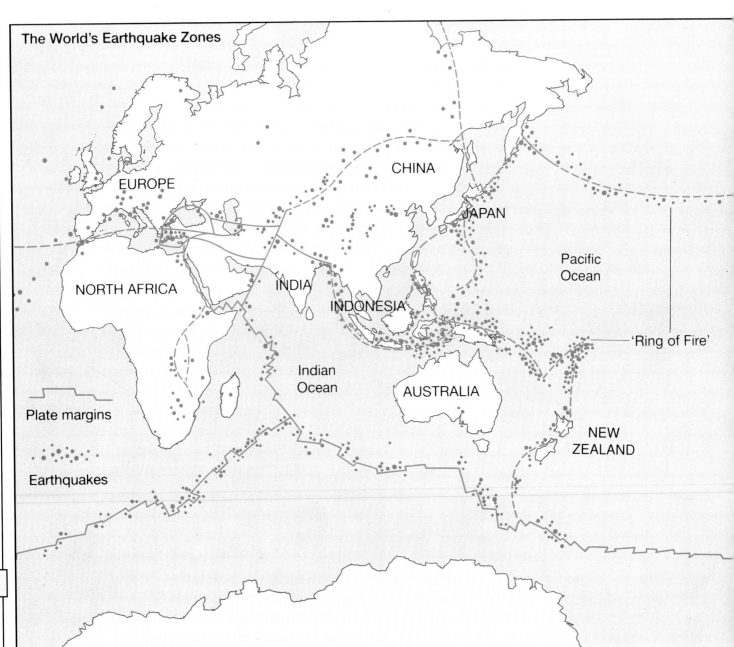

The World's Earthquake Zones

EUROPE

CHINA

JAPAN

Pacific Ocean

NORTH AFRICA

INDIA

INDONESIA

'Ring of Fire'

Indian Ocean

AUSTRALIA

Plate margins

NEW ZEALAND

Earthquakes

Left: Most plates meet beneath oceans and seas. But the San Andreas fault runs for 965 km along the western coast of California, USA.

'Ring of Fire'

Of all the earthquakes that have been recorded, most have occurred along the edge of the Pacific Plate. This plate follows the coastlines of the Far East and North and South America. It is known as the 'Ring of Fire' because of the volcanoes along its edge.

Other plates share boundaries across the Indian Ocean, through southern China, the Indian Himalayas and Iran, beneath the deserts of the Middle East, North Africa, the shores of the Mediterranean, and from the far reaches of the North Atlantic down to south of the Tropic of Capricorn.

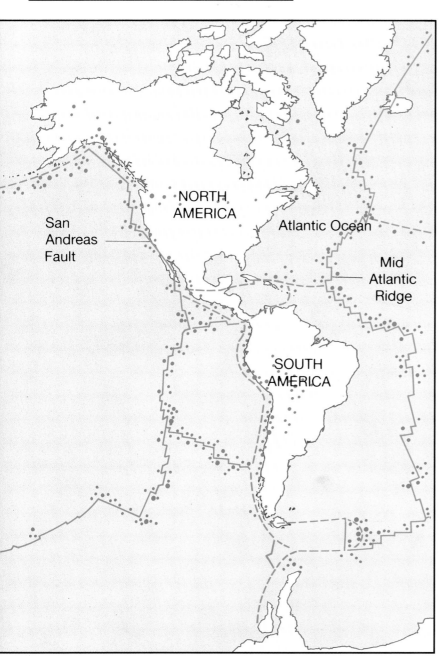

San Andreas Fault

NORTH AMERICA

Atlantic Ocean

Mid Atlantic Ridge

SOUTH AMERICA

Twentieth Century Earthquakes
(of over 10,000 deaths)

Date	Place	Deaths (in thousands)
1908	Italy	160
1920	China	180
1923	Japan	143
1935	India	60
1939	Turkey	40
1960	Morocco	12
1970	Peru	50
1972	Nicaragua	12
1976	China	700
1976	Guatemala	23
1988	Armenia	55
1990	Iran	35

THE EARTHQUAKE'S POWER

When earthquakes occur they can be devastating. The earth heaves and sways, rocks about and even splits open. However, the earth's movement usually lasts for only a few seconds.

Earthquakes vary enormously in strength. The total energy released by an earthquake is called its magnitude. Magnitude refers to the earthquake's size and is measured on the Richter scale by an instrument called a seismograph. Most earthquakes are between 3 and 8 in magnitude.

The shaking on the surface of the earth produced by an earthquake is called its intensity. This is measured on the Modified Mercalli scale and describes the amount of damage caused by an earthquake.

The damage caused
Earthquakes take place at depths down to about 600 km. The ones occurring between the earth's crust and 70 km into the earth are the most dangerous. The vibrations on the surface are often so powerful that buildings are shaken apart. More damage may follow when supplies of water, gas or electricity are cut off and fires break out.

An earthquake in March 1964 ripped open the earth at Anchorage in Alaska, breaking up gas and electrical power cables.

Magnitude (Richter Scale)	Intensity (Mercalli Scale)	Damage description (Very approximate)
4	5.5	Widely felt, plaster cracked
5	7	Strong vibration, weak buildings and chimneys damaged
6	8.5	Ordinary buildings badly damaged
7	10	Well built buildings destroyed
8	11.5	Specially designed buildings badly damaged
9	12	Widespread destruction

Landslides and tsunami

Earthquakes in mountainous and coastal regions can also cause other hazards. Landslides triggered by earthquakes have wiped out entire communities. In some coastal areas the effect of ground movements under the sea cause gigantic waves, called tsunami. These waves may sweep inland and cause havoc in places several kilometres from the coast.

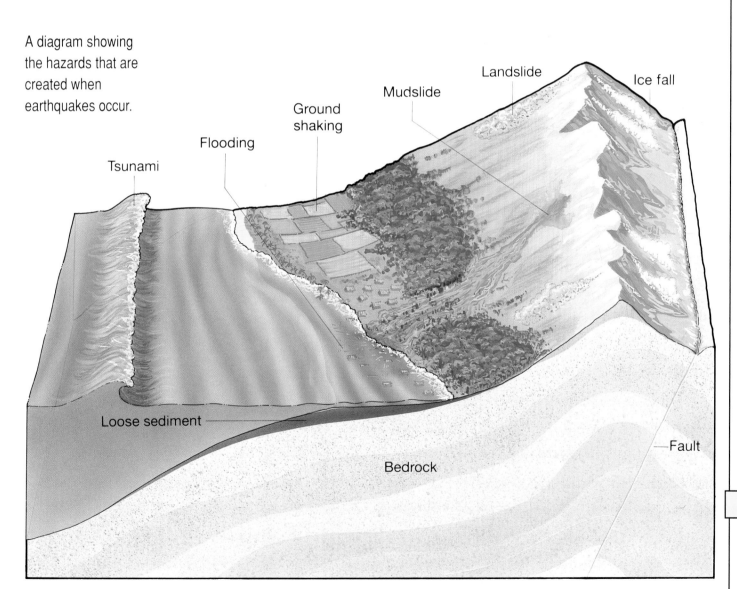

A diagram showing the hazards that are created when earthquakes occur.

Tsunami

Flooding

Ground shaking

Mudslide

Landslide

Ice fall

Loose sediment

Bedrock

Fault

Earthquakes in San Francisco

In the Americas, part of the Pacific Plate travels beneath the length of California in a 32 km-deep crack called the San Andreas Fault. The rocks on either side of the fault are under great strain. Stress is created as the Pacific Plate moves northwards about one centimetre per year, pushing against the North American Plate which thrusts southwards.

The plate suddenly moves

In 1906 the Pacific Plate suddenly moved 3 m north. This caused an earthquake in San Francisco which measured 8.25 on the Richter scale. It flattened a huge area of offices, shops and houses, and fractured gas mains

The damage to San Francisco at dawn on 18 April 1906 was devastating. After the earthquake destroyed a large part of the city, fire broke out.

'The moment I felt the house tremble ... I leaped out of bed and and rushed out to the front door ... I felt sure the house would fall before I got out. It rocked like a ship on a "rough sea". Streets of people ... poured into the streets ... a mourning, groaning, sobbing, wailing, weeping and praying crowd. The deathly air [was] very oppressive ... quiver after quiver followed... until it seemed as if the very heart of this old earth was broken and was throbbing and dying away slowly and gently.' (Eva Atkins Campbell, 1 May 1906.)

A house in San Francisco sagged sideways to the ground during the earthquake that bought widespread damage on 17 October 1989.

The Call=Chronicle=Examiner

SAN FRANCISCO, THURSDAY, APRIL 19, 1906.

EARTHQUAKE AND FIRE: SAN FRANCISCO IN RUINS

causing fires to start. About 700 Americans died, and 250,000 were made homeless in the disaster.

Waiting for disaster

For years afterwards, American scientists studied records, and forecasted that another major earthquake would happen in San Francisco. This was likely to be an even greater disaster because the city had grown bigger over the years.

The earthquake damage

The earthquake everyone expected finally happened at 5.04 pm on Tuesday, 17 October 1989, and measured 7.1 on the Richter scale. Luckily scientists were wrong about the huge numbers of casualties. The earthquake killed only 68 people in the city and its outlying areas. Out of three million people, 3,757 were injured – a low number for such a big city. But 1,400 homes had been destroyed and 27,000 businesses damaged. A year after the earthquake, more than one billion dollars had been spent repairing roads, homes and offices, with much more work still to be carried out in the city.

Mexico City

On 19 September 1985, Mexico City was rocked by an earthquake which measured 8.1 on the Richter scale. It demolished nearly half the capital in one of the greatest disasters to strike Central America this century.

The cause of the earthquake

Mexico's ordeal began 350 km west of the capital. The Cocos Plate, which moves beneath the lighter American Plate, snapped 20 km below the surface. This produced a massive earthquake which sent shock waves racing inland.

Rescuers shifting through a heap of concrete after the earthquake hit Mexico City in 1985.

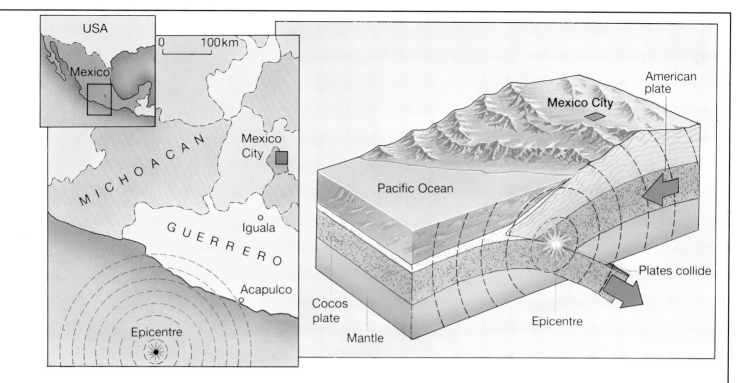

The cut-away diagram shows how two plates collide deep under the ground. Inset maps show the epicentre and position of the Mexico City earthquake.

The earthquake's violence

The first shocks were gentle warnings. Then, with tremendous violence and a roar like an express train hurtling along underground, the big one struck. In a few terrifying minutes, 7,000 Mexicans were killed and thousands more injured.

Hotels, schools, office blocks, cathedrals, churches and houses were flattened or tossed across streets. Skyscrapers swayed like trees caught in a hurricane, then collapsed, burying hundreds of people beneath them. A block of flats eight storeys high sank to a quarter of its size with much of its roof still in place. Some buildings which survived the shock were left leaning at dangerous angles.

'A mighty blow from hell'

'Mexico has been hit with the force of a mighty blow from hell', was how one television reporter described the earthquake, which brought rescue teams from Britain and the USA to explore the mountains of rubble to try to find trapped victims. A series of tremors lasted only a few minutes but transformed the centre of Mexico City into a ruin. It left thousands dead and many more thousands trapped in the rubble.

> *"The building started swaying all over the place before it collapsed. We just held on to each other and prayed."*
> *(Scott Thomason, American tourist.)*

Earthquakes that occur in any densely populated area like Mexico City usually cause great devastation as buildings are not earthquake-proof. On 28 July 1976, an earthquake focused on the highly populated industrial city of Tangshan in China.

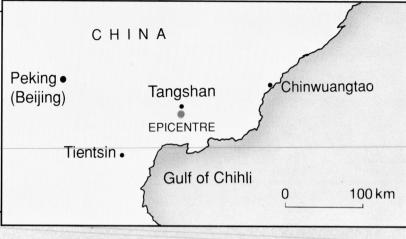

CHINA

Peking (Beijing) •

Tangshan
•
EPICENTRE

• Chinwuangtao

Tientsin •

Gulf of Chihli

0   100 km

Shock flattens Chinese city

Before an earthquake occurs, minor tremors are usually felt. But the earthquake in China arrived without warning. Between 650,000 and 750,000 people died as a shock of 8.3 on the Richter scale almost completely destroyed Tangshan. Buildings shook in the capital of Peking (Beijing), 160 km away. Strong tremors continued for several days. The remaining 100,000 residents fled to makeshift camps in the surrounding countryside. When the last tremor raced through the city, hardly a building was left standing, and all its coal mines had been flooded.

Rebuilding Tangshan

In rebuilding Tangshan, the city was planned so that all the apartment blocks, offices and factories were designed to resist earthquakes. Parks instead of homes were built on ground above the fault lines. Within two years, people were living and working in the city. By the early 1980s, the number of people in Tangshan was the same as before the earthquake struck.

This was one of the first photographs to be taken of Tangshan after the 1976 earthquake.

China's worst earthquakes

Year	Official deaths (in thousands)	Affected area
1290	100	China
1556	830	Shensi province
1668	50	Shantung province
1731	100	Peking (Beijing)
1739	50	China
1920	200	Kansu province
1927	40	Nan Mountains
1932	70	Kansu province
1970	10	S. Yunnan province

A rescue team searching for survivors trapped in the rubble at Spitak, in 1988.

'Spitak was in ruins. Schools, apartment buildings, grain elevators, a lift manufacturing plant reduced to rubble...' (Izvestia).

Armenian disaster

One of the strongest earthquakes ever recorded on the Richter scale took place in the Soviet Republic of Armenia, on 7 December 1988. Seismographs recorded a magnitude of nearly 7 as the shock flattened all the buildings taller than eight storeys high in the city of Leninakan. Huge cracks appeared in the road to Spitak a town with a population of 20,000 inhabitants which was described as 'utterly destroyed'. Officially 55,000 people died in the two towns although many thousands more are belived to have been killed.

Rescue attempts

After the earthquake struck, survivors wandered stunned through city streets, many gathering around campfires for warmth. Soldiers set up tent

cities for people from devastated regions. They tried to restore electricity and water supplies but lack of equipment prevented officials from launching a proper rescue operation.

Officials needed heavy machines like bulldozers that could clear the streets of rubble, but these were not available. This meant that ambulances were not able to reach injured victims. Fortunately, Western countries came to their help by sending in fleets of aircraft carrying relief supplies for the 500,000 homeless who had only tents for shelter in the freezing temperatures.

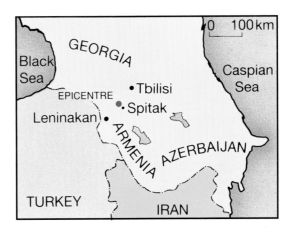

Below: Pre-fabricated buildings for earthquake survivors are unloaded from a cargo aircraft.

For hundreds of years, scientists have been looking for ways to predict major earthquakes. Today, research is carried out by seismologists throughout the world, especially in China, Japan, the USSR and the USA.

Earthquake prediction is still in its early days. Knowing when earthquakes are likely to happen still baffles scientists everywhere. Minor tremors are sometimes followed by a big shock, but often they are not. The really big earthquake can and does happen without warning.

Seismic activity

Every day dozens of earthquakes are registered on seismographs in

A seismograph recording minor tremors on a seismogram as part of a constant world-wide watch on earthquakes.

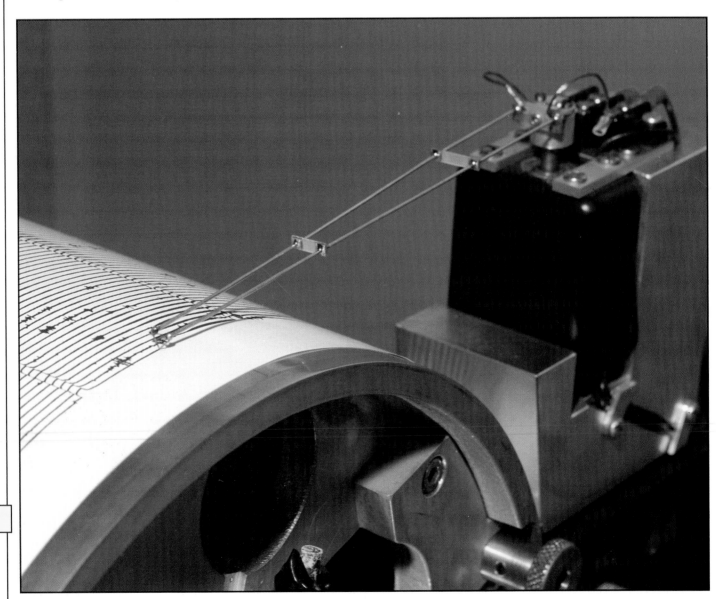

a world-wide network of stations. The seismograph is a sensitive instrument that can detect small shocks deep below the surface. By timing when the waves arrive, scientists can tell how far away the earthquake is and where its epicentre lies.

American scientists say that big earthquakes can be predicted if seismic activity increases over many years. They discovered that this happened in the years leading up to the San Francisco earthquakes of 1906, 1968 and 1989. But at other times seismographs were not able to predict earthquakes, such as before the Tangshan earthquake of 1986.

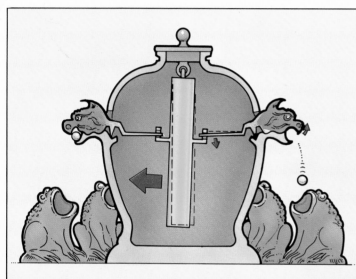

Early recordings

The world's first instrument for measuring earthquakes was developed in China in the second century. A pendulum hung in a bronze vessel, which moved when an earthquake occurred. This caused one of the eight dragon mechanisms on the vessel to vibrate, so a ball fell out of its mouth and was caught by one of the toads underneath. This indicated the direction the seismic wave had come from.

The modern seismograph

Todays scientific recorders pick up the waves of energy from an earthquake and record the results on a seismogram.
The device has a base that shakes with the earthquake. A pen is attached to a hanging weight, which remains still. The movements of the base cause the pen to record the vertical movements (1) and the horizontal movements (2) as graphs.

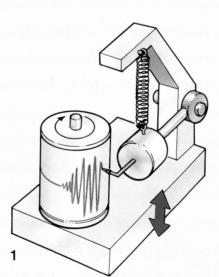

1

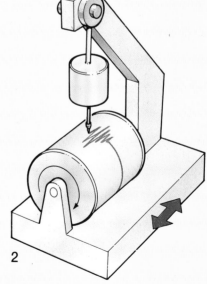

2

Surveying equipment

Some parts of the world are constantly monitored for earthquakes using sophisticated equipment. This equipment records the changing levels of the land and the sea, and any changes in the movement or the make-up of rocks. The slightest movement in the earth's crust is detected by an American satellite known as LAGEOS. This stands for 'Laser Geodynamic Satellite'. It spins around the earth in orbit at nearly 6,000 km high. It has 426 prisms (or 'eyes') on its dimpled surface which note the tiniest shifts in the positions of the earth's plates. It will stay in orbit for many years.

Earthquakes are detected by using a variety of equipment.

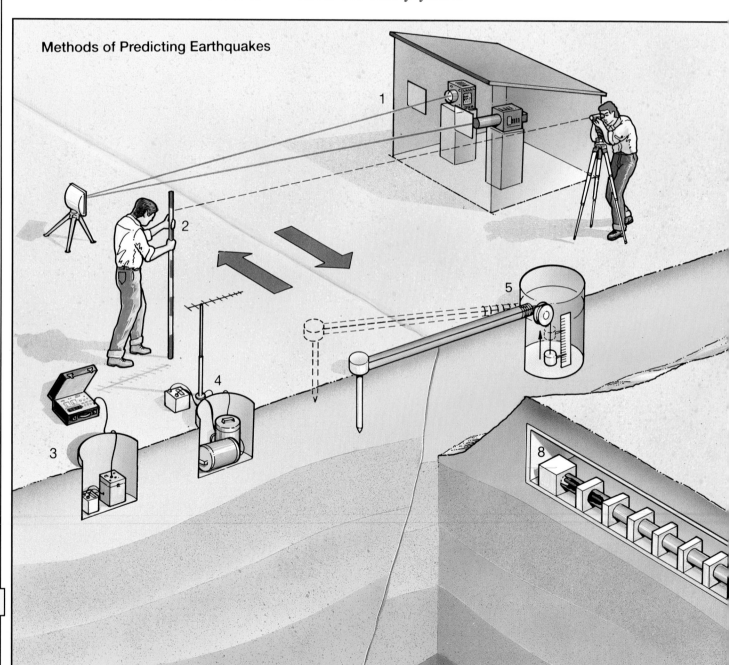

Methods of Predicting Earthquakes

Natural indicators

Scientists still have a long way to go before they can predict earthquakes successfully, but some people have seen strange happenings which tells them that an earthquake is about to occur. In the winter of 1988 people living in Quebec in Canada, saw a spectacular display of natural fireworks. Some looked like fireballs in the sky and they spurted a luminous spray at night. Others lit up houses, trees and clouds with yellow-orange light and coloured rays appeared in the sky. Geologists checked the reports of these sightings with seismic records and found that the lights had appeared when a series of tremors had occurred.

In China it has been found that animals are able to sense vibrations in the earth before people. Snakes emerge from their holes in freezing weather, rats leave their buildings, while dogs and cats shiver and sometimes run about like ants.

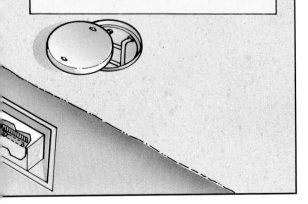

1. Observatory with laser equipment
2. Surveys to show changes in land level
3. Measuring changes in the earth's magnetic field
4. Recording earthquakes on a seismograph
5. Measuring the speed rocks move past each other
6. Measuring changes in land level
7. Measuring the earth's gravity
8. Measuring strain on rocks

Below: Scientists in the 1970s preparing to launch the satellite LAGEOS, which records underground plate movements.

RELIEF AND RESCUE

In recent years, many nations have joined in relief and rescue operations after major disasters have occurred. Governments have given large sums of money. Charities have sent out people carrying medical supplies, food, clothing and bedding to devastated areas.

Special help
The International Rescue Corps (IRC) was formed in Britain in 1980 after an earthquake hit southern Italy, killing 3,000 people. The IRC carries medicine, relief supplies, radio

Left below: The sequence of events following an earthquake.

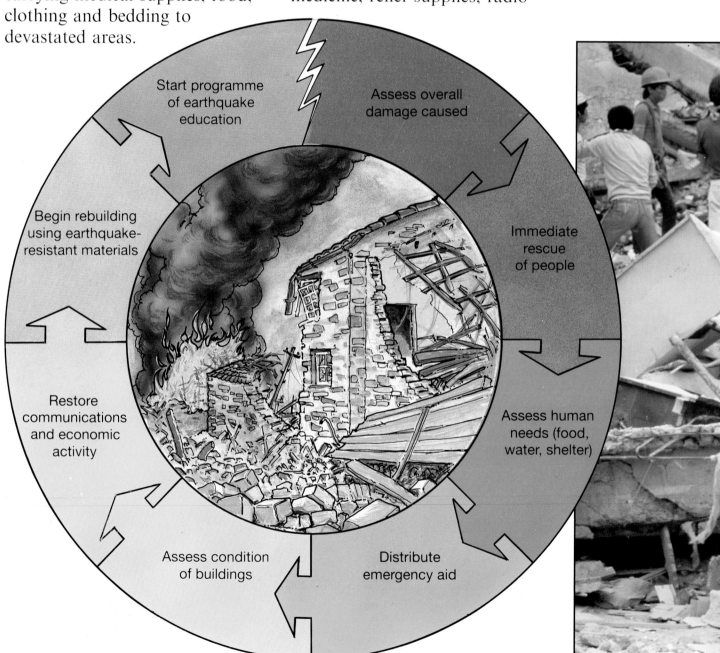

Start programme of earthquake education

Assess overall damage caused

Begin rebuilding using earthquake-resistant materials

Immediate rescue of people

Restore communications and economic activity

Assess human needs (food, water, shelter)

Assess condition of buildings

Distribute emergency aid

The Red Cross are the official rescue team here at the scene of an earthquake. They carry basic life-saving equipment with them.

equipment and machines that can detect people trapped in disaster-hit regions. The volunteers are on standby for 24 hours a day and work closely with governments, the United Nations, the Red Cross and relief organizations.

Clearing up

Specialist teams from the United Nations, the USA, Canada and European countries have also taken part in clearing away the wreckage, restoring water, gas and electricity and telling people how they can re-build their homes. Survivors of an earthquake often do not want to move away from the earthquake region that has always been their home. Many towns flattened by earthquakes have risen again and again on the same spot.

PREVENTING EARTHQUAKE DAMAGE

One way to reduce the loss of life caused by earthquakes is to predict when they will occur and then move everybody who is at risk out of the area. Another way is to make sure that buildings they live in are sited, designed and built so as to resist the earthquake's tremors.

Today scientists are able to pinpoint the areas that are most likely to be hit by earthquakes.

This timber framed building fell down because it was not firmly fixed to its foundations.

These buildings have been designed to resist earthquakes.

Most of these areas lie along fault lines, and in places where the ground can be rocked by vibrations. When a big earthquake occurs, planners could think about rebuilding the town in a new and safer location. But more often they will try to find ways of rebuilding it in the same place and making it as earthquake-proof as possible.

Building design

Buildings can be designed so that the impact of the earthquake is lessened. For instance, it has been found that buildings made from wood are less likely to fall down than ones made of brick, but they must stand on solid ground. A light roof does not cause as much damage when it falls as one made from heavy tiles. All buildings need to stand on solid rock or have firm foundations.

Buildings need to 'give' when the earth vibrates so they must be flexible. Skyscrapers built with steel frames will sway from side to side without falling because of their flexibility.

Preventing destruction

It is not possible to make some areas of the world totally earthquake-proof, but it is hoped the damage can be lessened as much as possible to prevent any more major disasters occurring in the future.

PROJECTS

1. Project Challenge

Survivors of earthquakes urgently need shelter, and tents are often not suitable for extremes of climate. Can you design a better unit to be made from low-cost materials?

Remember that emergency supplies are usually air-freighted to disaster sites, but since large planes cannot always land, the cargoes are unloaded as the plane flies slowly to the ground. Space is vital so your unit must flat pack and be simple to assemble with no special tools.

Materials:
Cereal cartons
Adhesive tape and fasteners
Note pad and pencil
Scissors

Method:

1. List your basic needs for survival. Discuss these with others.

2. Sketch some ideas for a shelter. Draw a plan of what you think your model will look like.

3. Build your model from stiff card very carefully to scale.

4. Decide what should go inside your shelter.

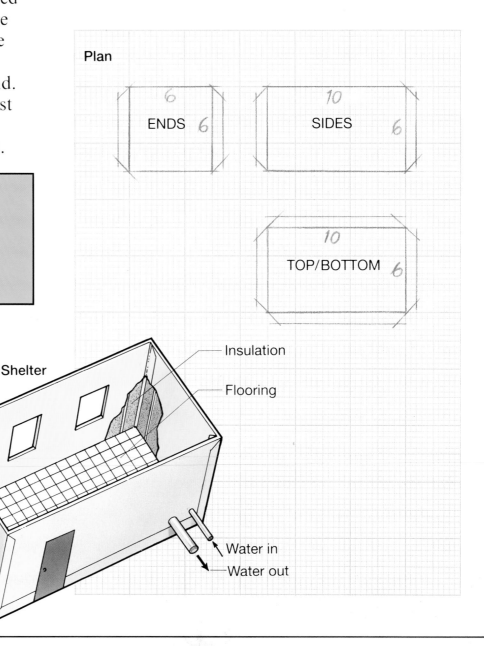

Plan

ENDS 6 6

SIDES 10 6

TOP/BOTTOM 10 6

Portable Toilet

Water out
Water in
Ventilation
Power supply

Shelter

Insulation
Flooring

Water in
Water out

2. Lightweight houses for earthquake zones

In regions where earthquakes are common, buildings are made from lightweight materials that allow the whole structure to be flexible. In Japan, timber is used for a framework and then covered with thin boarding or tensioned paper screen. This allows for ground movement, and is less dangerous if violent tremors cause the building to collapse.

Method:

1. Decide on the type of house that you would like to build.

2. Make the walls of your house. Cut the straws to length and fix to a pin board. Glue cardboard triangles to the corners and leave to dry.

3. When the wall frames are dry, cover them with tissue paper and glue in place. When the glue is dry, spray the tissue with water to tension it. Assemble the walls with strips of adhesive tape.

4. Cut a piece of card to the roof size. Score and fold for the ridge. Stick strips of straws on to the roof and when dry, fix to the walls with adhesive tape.

Materials:
Art straws
Waterproof glue
Thin card
Tissue paper
Adhesive tape
Pin board and pins
Plant mist spray with clean water

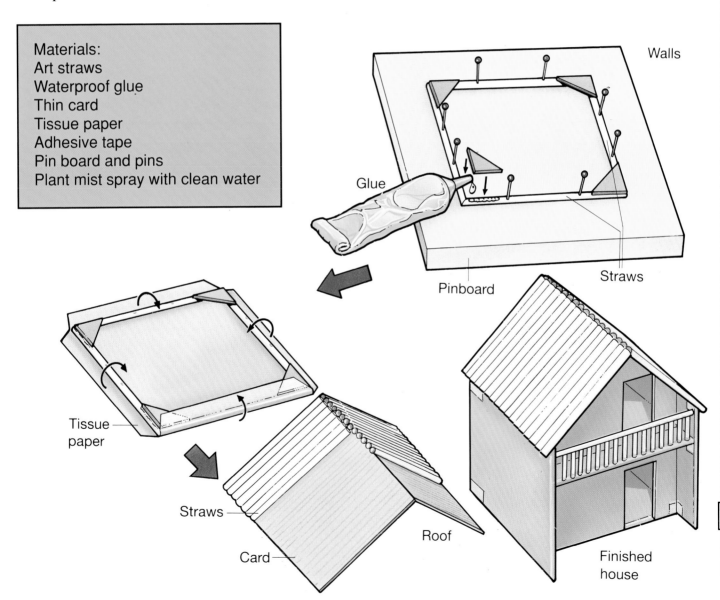

Walls

Glue

Pinboard

Straws

Tissue paper

Straws

Card

Roof

Finished house

29

GLOSSARY

CRUST The layer of rock at the earth's surface.

EPICENTRE The position on the earth's surface above the focus of an earthquake.

FAULT A large crack or break in a series of rocks. This is where two parts of the earth can slip past each other.

GEOLOGIST A scientist who studies the origin, history, structure and processes of the earth.

INFERNO A huge, roaring fire.

LANDSLIDE When loose rock and soil slides down a steep slope.

LUMINOUS Radiating light.

MAGNITUDE The size of an earthquake as measured on the Richter scale.

PLATES Giant slabs of underground rocks, often bigger than continents.

RED CROSS The international organization formed to care for the sick, wounded and homeless in wartime and also during natural disasters.

RELIEF SUPPLIES Cargoes of food, water, medicines, clothing, tents and huts sent to disaster areas.

RICHTER SCALE A mathematical scale that is used to show the size of an earthquake.

SATELLITE A human-made object circling the earth.

SHOCK WAVES The waves of energy that are produced underground as rocks snap. When they reach the surface they cause violent shaking.

STRESS Energy that is created when two forces work against each other.

TREMORS The shaking caused by earthquakes.

TSUNAMI A large sea wave, sometimes called a tidal wave, caused by an earthquake.

VIBRATION A continuous shaking movement.

BOOKS TO READ

The Active Earth
by David Lambert (Methuen, 1981)

Earthquake
by Brian Knapp (Macmillan, 1989)

Earthquakes and Volcanoes
by Martyn Bramwell (Franklin Watts, 1986)

Earthquakes and Volcanoes
by David Lambert (Wayland, 1980)

Earthquakes and Volcanoes
by Sara Steel (A & C Black, 1982)

Mountains and Earth Movements
by Iain Bain (Wayland, 1984)

The San Francisco Earthquake
by John Dudman (Wayland, 1988)

Picture acknowledgements

The publishers would like to thank the following for allowing their photographs to be reproduced in this book: Associated Press/Topham *cover*, 19 (right); Colorific! 14 (Alon Reininger/Contact), 24/25 (Frank Fournier/Contact); Frank Lane Picture Agency 10; Photri 12, 13, 23, 27; Picturepoint Ltd 4/5 (both); Science Photo Library 2/3 (Peter Menzel), 9 (David Parker), 20 (Tom McHugh), 26 bottom (Peter Menzel); Frank Spooner Pictures Ltd 16/17,18/19.

INDEX